Harp
Studies & Exercises
for Trinity College London exams from 2013

Initial–Grade 8

Published by
Trinity College London Press Ltd
trinitycollege.com

Registered in England
Company no. 09726123

Copyright © 2013 Trinity College London
Fifth impression, November 2021

Unauthorised photocopying is illegal
No part of this publication may be copied or reproduced in any
form or by any means without the prior permission of the publisher.

Cover image courtesy of Salvi Harps, Italy
Printed in England by Caligraving Ltd

Foreword

These studies and exercises have been designed for use in Trinity College London Harp and Non-pedal Harp exams. Short exercises accompany scales and arpeggios together as the first of the two Technical Work options whilst longer studies form the second option.

For details of current specific requirements for each grade see trinitycollege.com
In the event of any discrepancy of detail, the website overrides guidance given in this book.

The purpose of these studies and exercises and the Technical Work section of a Trinity exam is to encourage the development of the necessary wide range of technical skills for the performance of pieces. Players should aim for accuracy at an appropriate tempo with even control of rhythm and tone.

These studies and exercises are neither intended to be a teaching manual for harp, nor necessarily to indicate the level at which a particular technique should be introduced. Accordingly, grade levels have been omitted from this volume.

Most of the studies and exercises are suitable for both harps with pedals or without, but some studies are specifically indicated for pedal or non-pedal harps.

Pedal Harp

Pedal harp requirements are based on an instrument with 46 or 47 strings although most studies are playable on an instrument with a smaller range.

Non-pedal (Lever) Harp

Non-pedal harp requirements and lever harp settings are based on a 34 string instrument tuned in E♭. Harps tuned in other keys such as A♭ may also be used but lever settings and changes will need to be adjusted accordingly. Lever settings are given only when they are in addition to, or contrary to the key signature.

Players with single-action or triple harps may choose either lever or pedal harp studies or exercises depending on the chromatic suitability for the instrument.

Where an instrument lacks the highest or lowest strings used, a pragmatic response may be accepted, provided that it does not lessen the technical demands of the study or exercise.

Dynamics and phrasing

Intentionally there are minimal performance directions such as dynamics and phrasing to give the player the opportunity to make their own musical judgements, although where a specific dynamic is written, it should be followed. Higher marks are given for attention to musical shaping and the promptness and confidence of delivery.

Metronome Marks

Please note that these are *minimum* acceptable tempi – faster tempi may well give more musically convincing results.

Fingering

Fingering given are often an integral part of the technique on which each study or exercise focuses and should be followed unless adaptations are necessary e.g. due to physical limitations. Where no fingerings are given, please form your own judgement.

Notes on notation

⊕	étouffé sign
(♯∘)	lever change sign
G♯	pedal change sign
Fingering	1 = thumb, 2 = forefinger etc.
Harmonics	these are notated for the string on which they are to be played and sound an octave higher
Harmonics at the 12th	these are notated for the string on which they are to be played and sound an octave plus a perfect 5th higher
L.H./R.H.	left hand/right hand

Contents

Exercises

1. Swinging 5
2. Small Scissors 5
3. Big Scissors 5
4. Zebra Crossing 5
5. Why did the Chicken Cross the Road? 6
6. Stilts 6
7. Oceans Eight 6
8. Sliding Down 6
9. Hard as Nails 7
10. Popcorn 7
11. Bluesy 7
12. Sliding Up 7
13. A Bit Jazzy 8
14. Rocking Chair 8
15. PDLT 9
16. 4, 3, 2, Strong! 9
17. Impressive Twiddles 10
18. Waterfall 10
19. Put it Back 11
20. Smooth as Silk 11
21. Identical Twins 11
22. Smooth and Wide 12
23. Cross Fingers 12
24. More Cross Fingers 13
25. Psychotriller (pedal harp) 13
26. Psychotriller (non-pedal harp) 13
27. Sliding Low 14
28. Hairy Slides 14

Studies

29. Open the Show! 15
30. Tapestry 16
31. Bears in a Cage 17
32. Neat Pairs 18
33. Fanfare 19
34. Rodeo 20
35. A Grand Event 21
36. Get the Ball Rolling 22
37. Chimes Across the Fields 23
38. Cogwheels 24
39. Rocking Horse 25
40. A New Replacement 26
41. Hymn 27
42. Sailing the Isles 28
43. On Parade 29
44. The Watermill 30
45. Wallabies 31
46. Chinese Kites 32
47. Scales in the Desert 33
48. Scales in the Mountains 34
49. Camel Ride 35
50. Ditto! 36
51. Floating 37
52. Goldfish 38
53. Shining Scales 39
54. Down Under 40
55. Cool Dude 41
56. In a Hammock 42
57. Spooky Strings 43
58. Colour Changes 44
59. Bells 45
60. Elizabeth's Revel 46
61. Reflections 47
62. The Elegant Drawing Room 48
63. Mind your own Business 49
64. Going East 50
65. Lever it Up 52
66. Pedalling Up and Down Hill 53
67. An Ornamental Tune 54
68. Middle of the Irish Sea 55
69. Showing Off! 56
70. A Firm Fist 57
71. Two into One 59
72. Chunky Glisses 60
73. The Sea 61
74. Turning & Triliant 66
75. Weaving In and Out 68
76. Paired Bells 70
77. Hommage 71
78. Careful Whisper 74
79. I'm a B-Lever 77
80. Very Cross Fingering 80
81. Flashing Levers 82
82. Incy Wincy Slider 84

1. Swinging – for arpeggio patterns

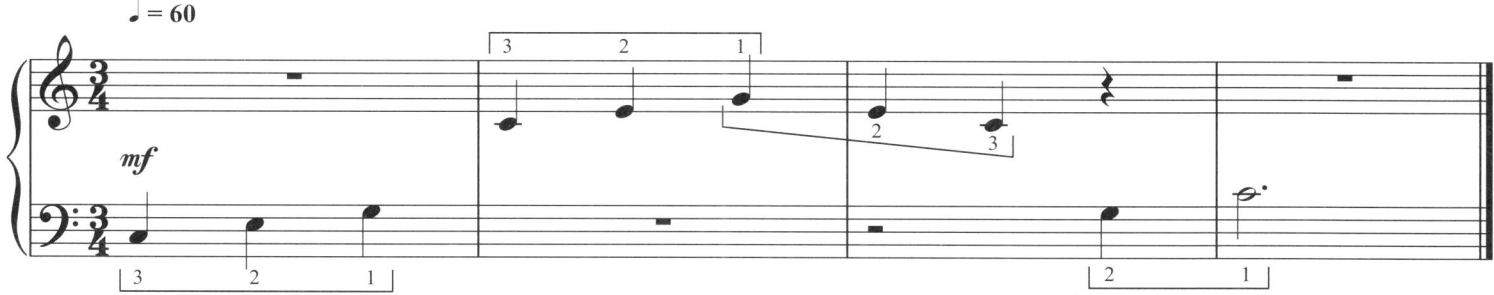

2. Small Scissors – for playing in thirds

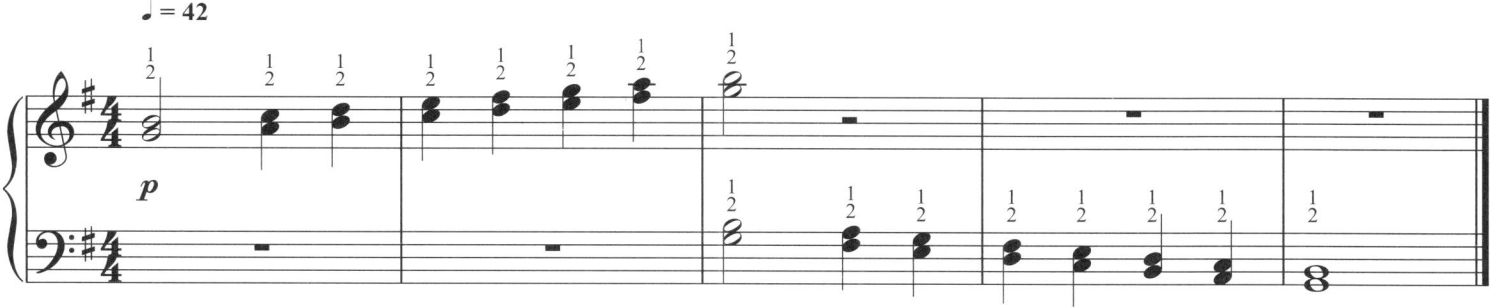

3. Big Scissors – for playing in sixths

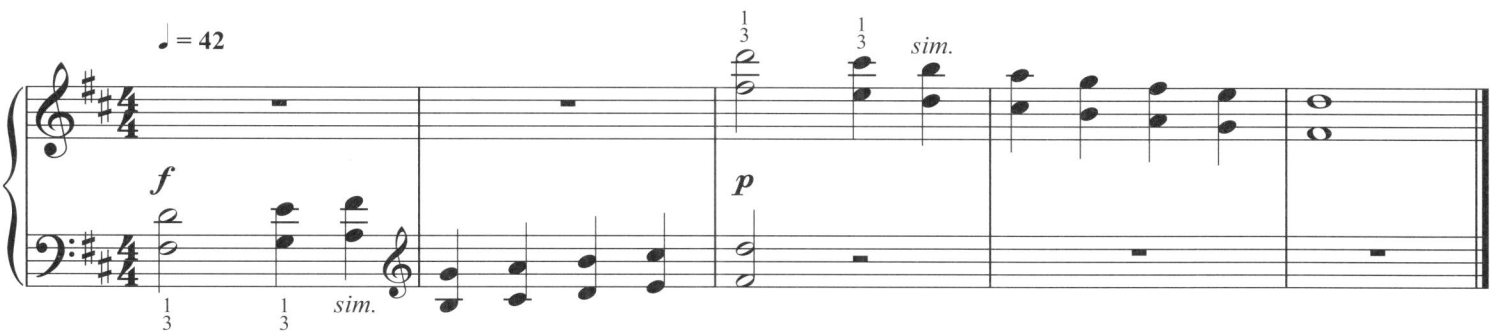

4. Zebra Crossing – for turning under and over loudly

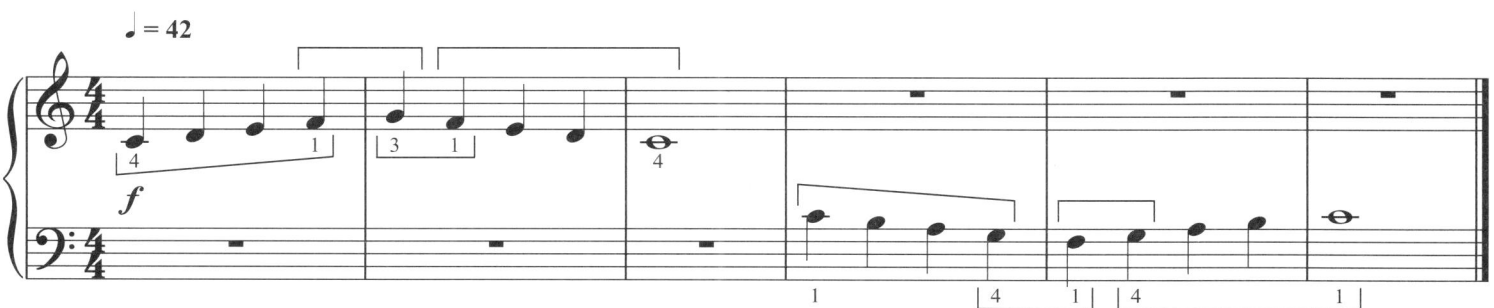

5. Why did the Chicken Cross the Road? – for turning under and over softly

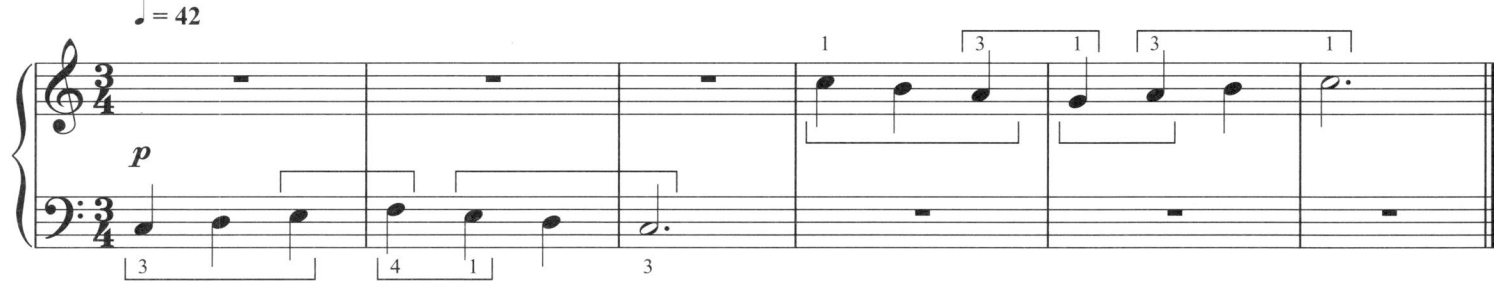

6. Stilts – for playing octaves in one hand

7. Oceans Eight – for arpeggio patterns in inversions

8. Sliding Down – for sliding the thumb

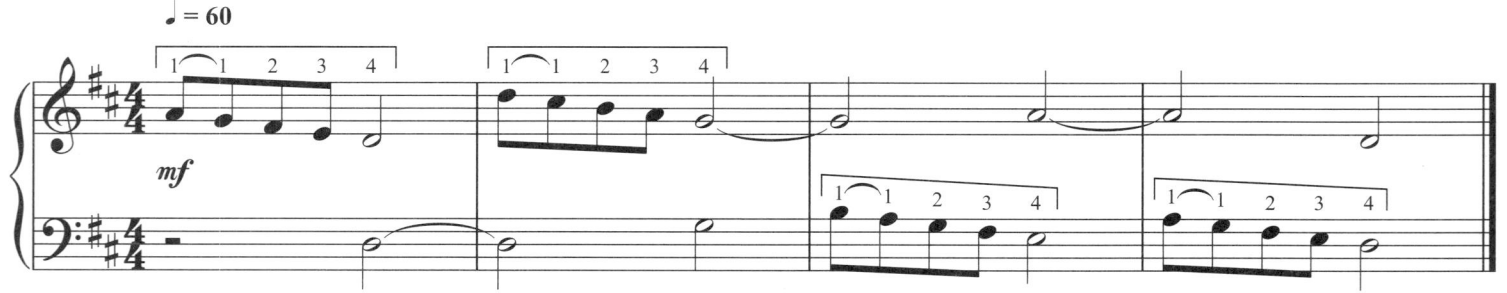

9. Hard as Nails – for use of the fingernail

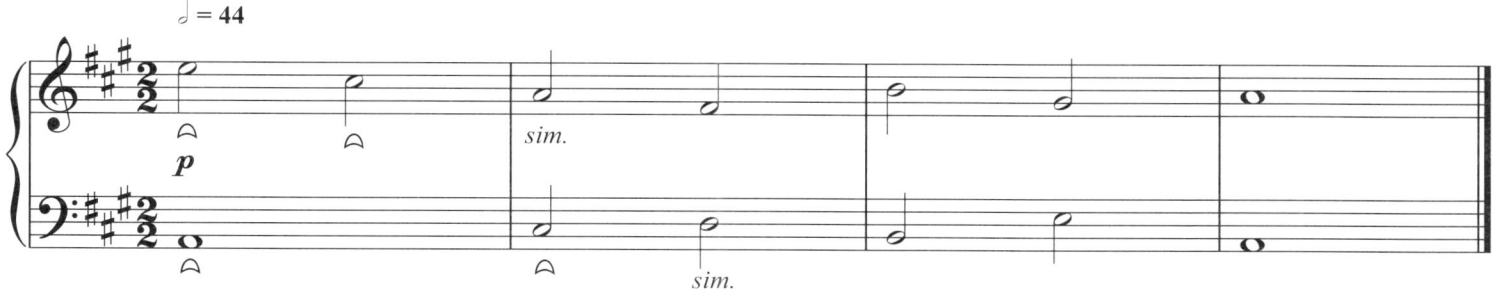

10. Popcorn – for staccato playing

11. Bluesy – for étouffés in the left hand

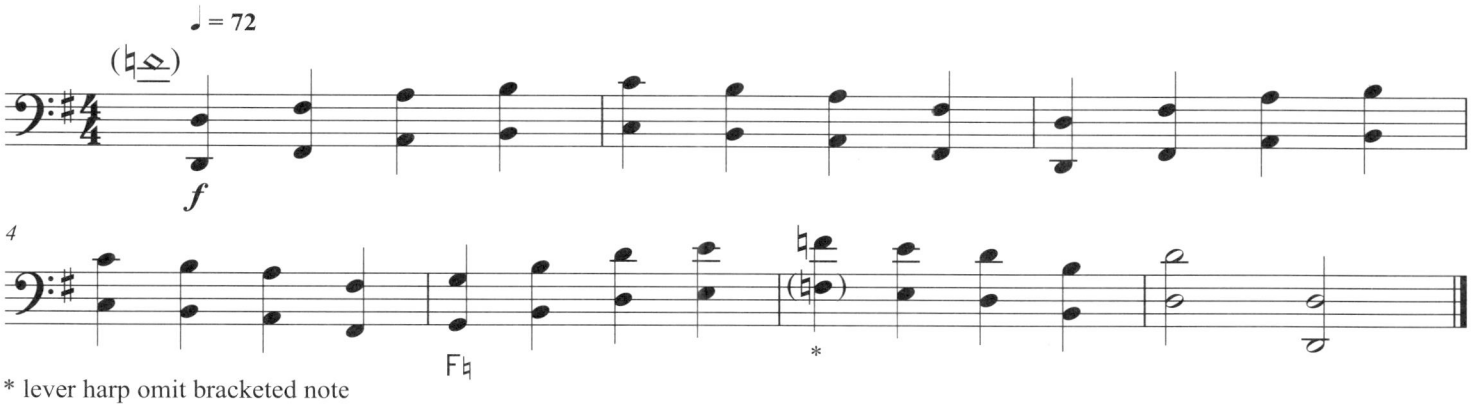

* lever harp omit bracketed note

12. Sliding Up – for sliding the 4th finger

13. A Bit Jazzy – for étouffés and pedal/lever glissandi

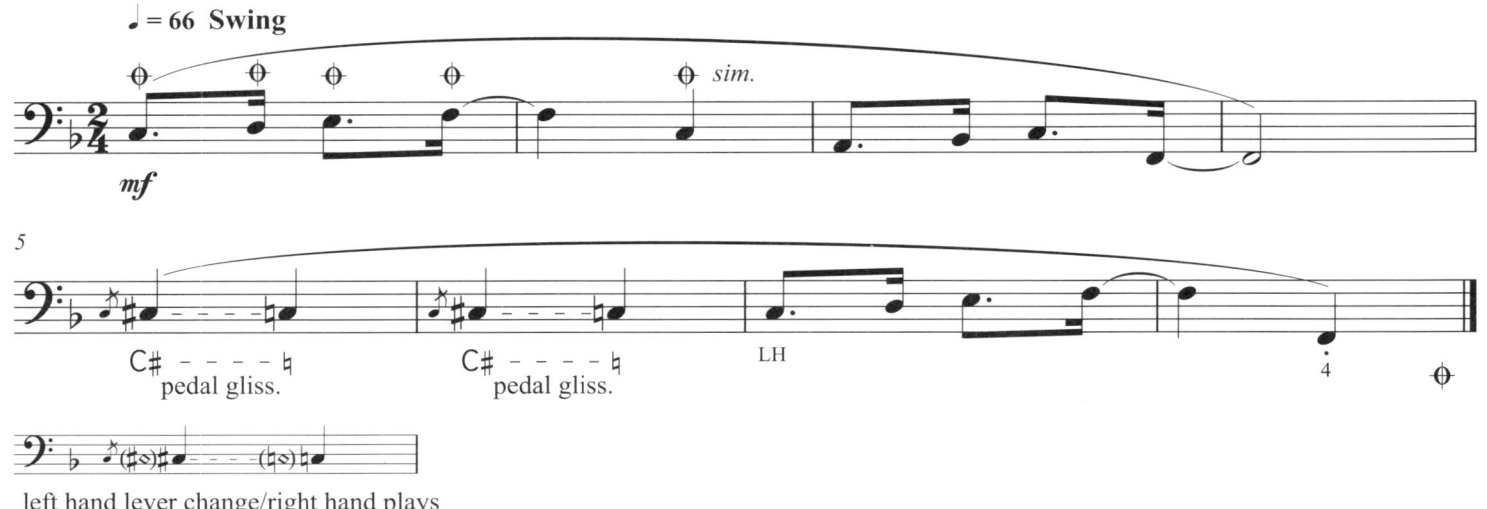

14. Rocking Chair – for finger articulation and thumb placing

15. PDLT – for près de la table

16. 4, 3, 2, Strong! – for finger strengthening, evenness and articulation

17. Impressive Twiddles – for mordents

18. Waterfall – for cantabile right thumb

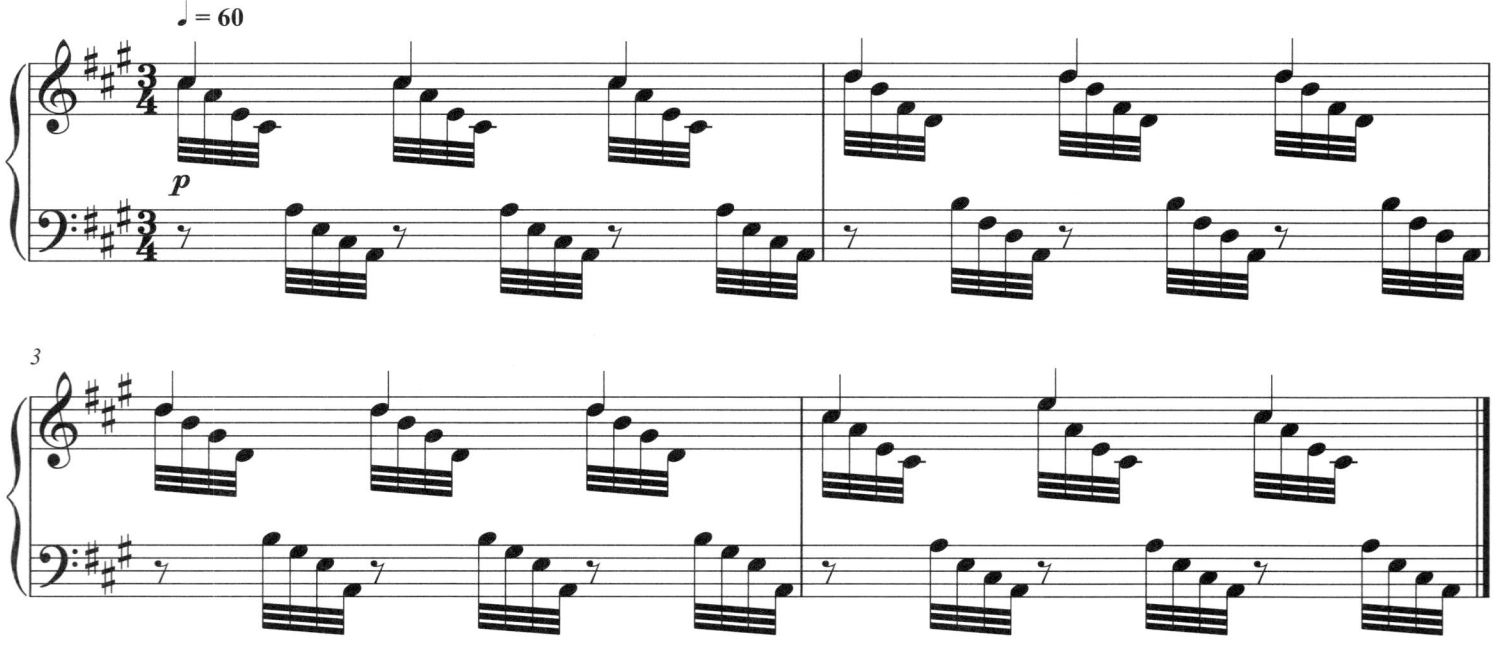

19. Put it Back – for staccato by replacing fingers

20. Smooth as Silk – for legato thirds sliding right-hand thumb

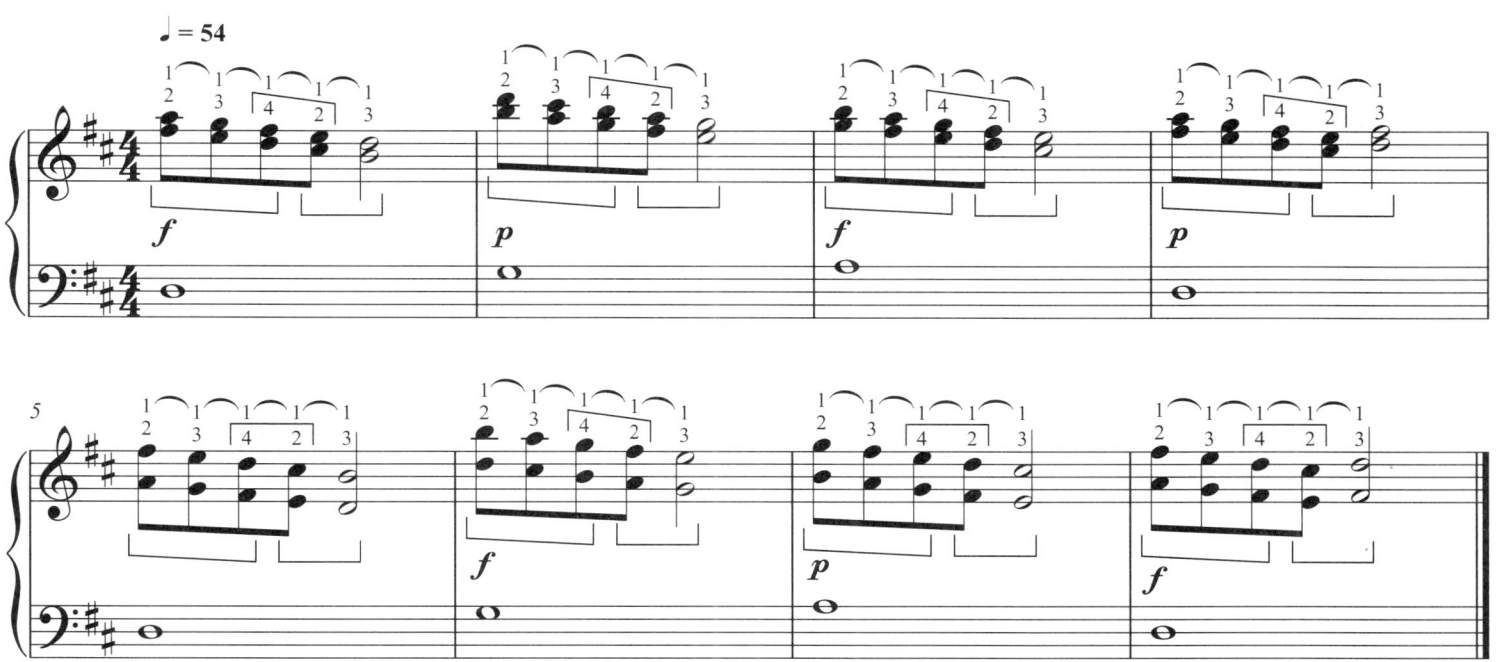

21. Identical Twins – for clearly articulated repeated notes using harmonics

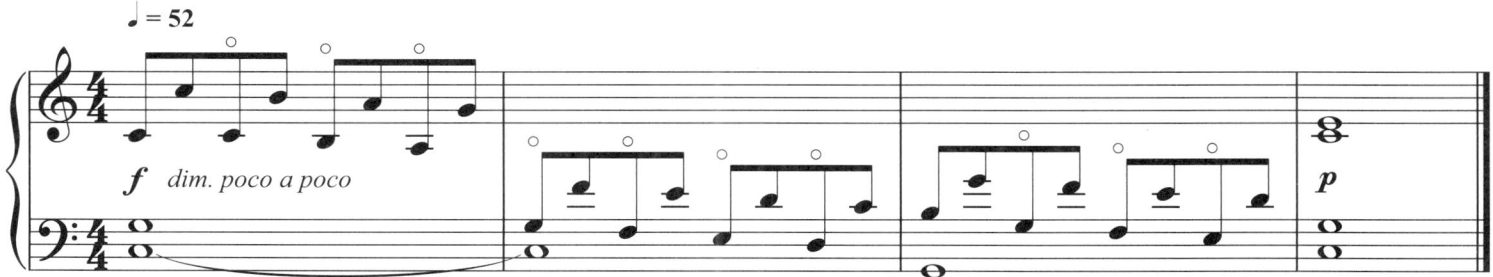

22. Smooth and Wide – for legato octaves with sliding thumb

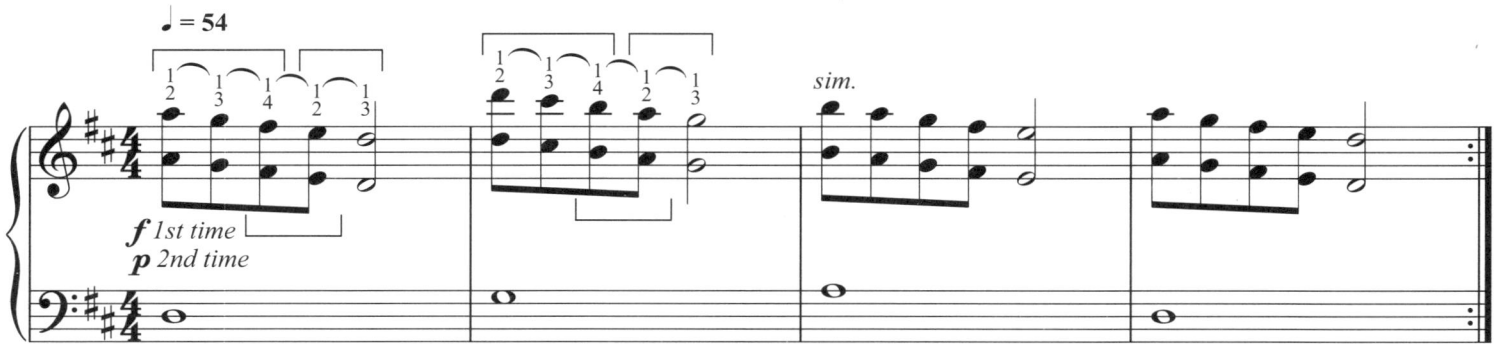

23. Cross Fingers – for cross-fingering 3-4 and 1-2

24. More Cross Fingers – for cross-fingering 2-4 and 1-3

25. Psychotriller (pedal harp) – for right hand trill and crossing left hand over right

26. Psychotriller (non-pedal harp) – for right hand trill and crossing left hand over right

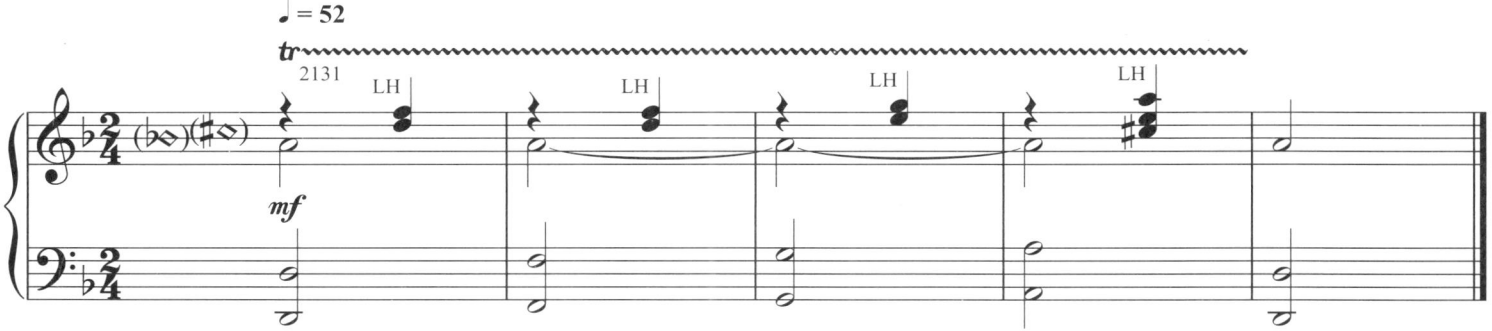

27. Sliding Low – for left hand legato sixths and octaves with sliding thumb

28. Hairy Slides – for mordents and slides

29. Open the Show!

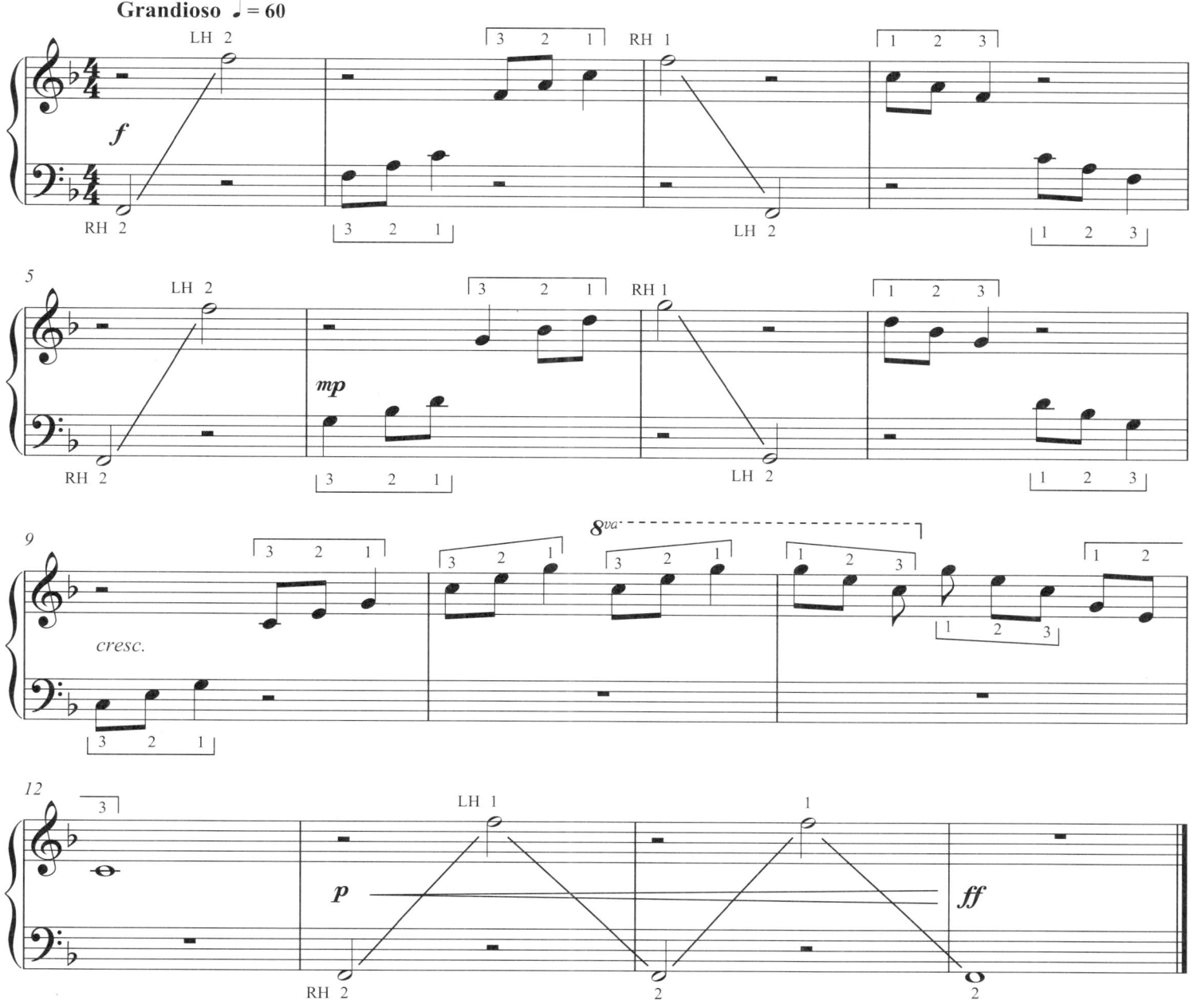

Try experimenting with different dynamics to capture a grand and dramatic opening to a magical event!

For an even tone and dynamic, keep the pressure even on the strings right to the end of each glissando.

TIP: for a stronger, louder sound, slightly hook your 2nd finger or thumb.

30. Tapestry

Experiment with tapping different parts of the soundboard or different parts of the harp. Listen to the difference in the sound.

TIP: for a nice resonant tap, use the knuckle of the 3rd finger somewhere in the middle of the soundboard.

31. Bears in a Cage

TIP: place fingers cleanly onto the strings to avoid buzzing – especially on the wire strings – and squeeze the strings a little firmly before releasing them.

32. Neat Pairs

TIP: for a rounder sound, make sure that your 2nd finger pulls right into the curve of your palm when it plays, until it actually touches your palm. Thumbs bend right over the hands. Hands themselves remain stable and still when the fingers play. Make sure fingernails are not too long so they do not catch the strings.

33. Fanfare

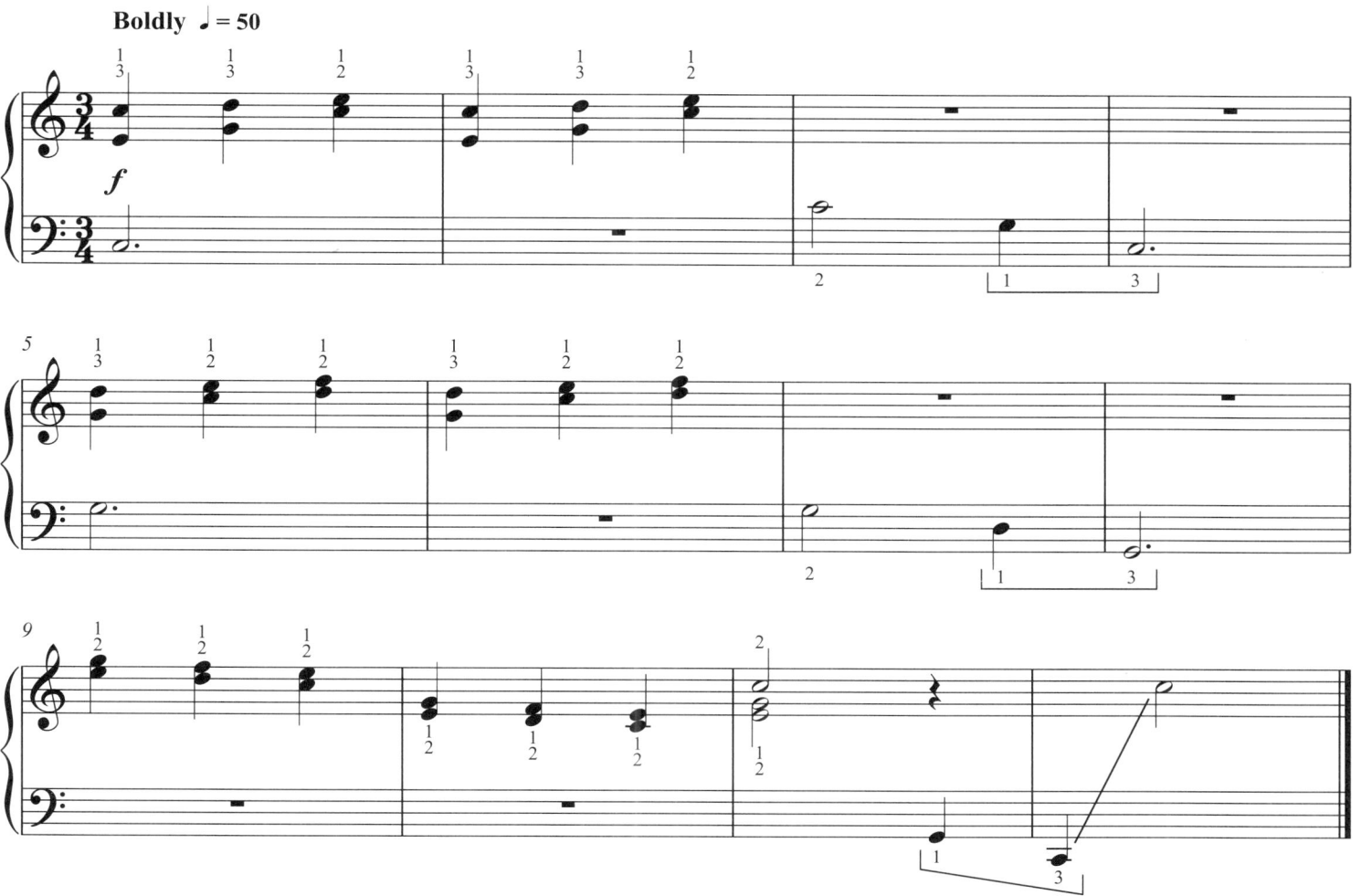

TIP: the right-hand chords in each of the first two bars form what is known as a 'horn passage'. Make sure that these chords are exactly together as well as having steady rhythm and even tone throughout.

34. Rodeo

TIP: don't forget that the metronome speed given here is a minimum. You can give a much more energetic feeling if you play faster – but it still needs to be even and steady!

35. A Grand Event

Even though this should be loud and grand, the sound should be rounded and not ugly. Listen carefully to ensure this.

TIP: mentally divide each beat into three from the start so you will know how the triplets should sound. That way, you will keep the beat steady.

36. Get the Ball Rolling

Fix B♭s, F♯s & G♯s throughout

Smooth & Flowing ♩ = 96

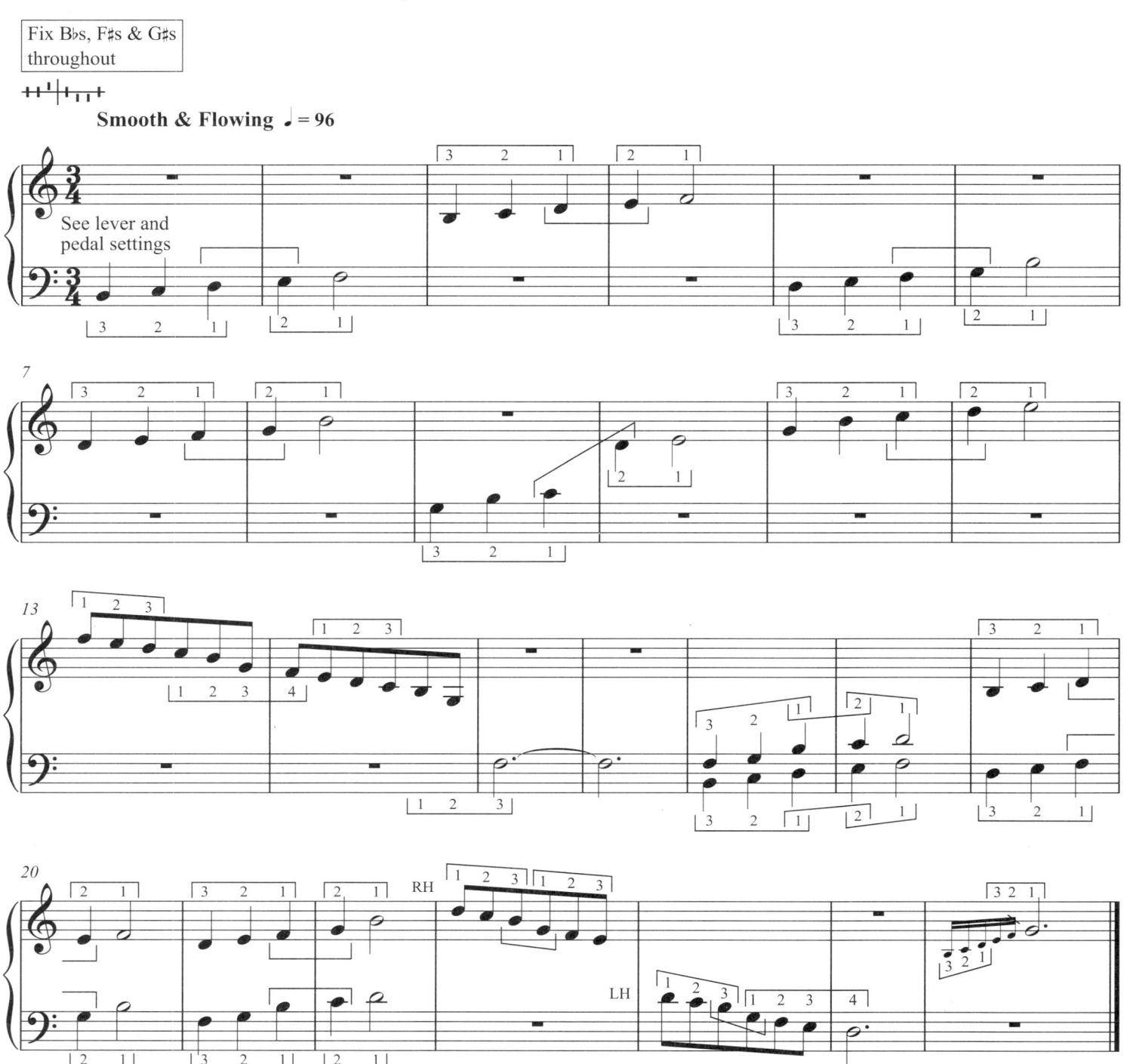

Add your own musical shaping and dynamics.
When turning under, the notes should be smooth and even.

TIP: keep the hand and wrist stable when turning under.

37. Chimes Across the Fields

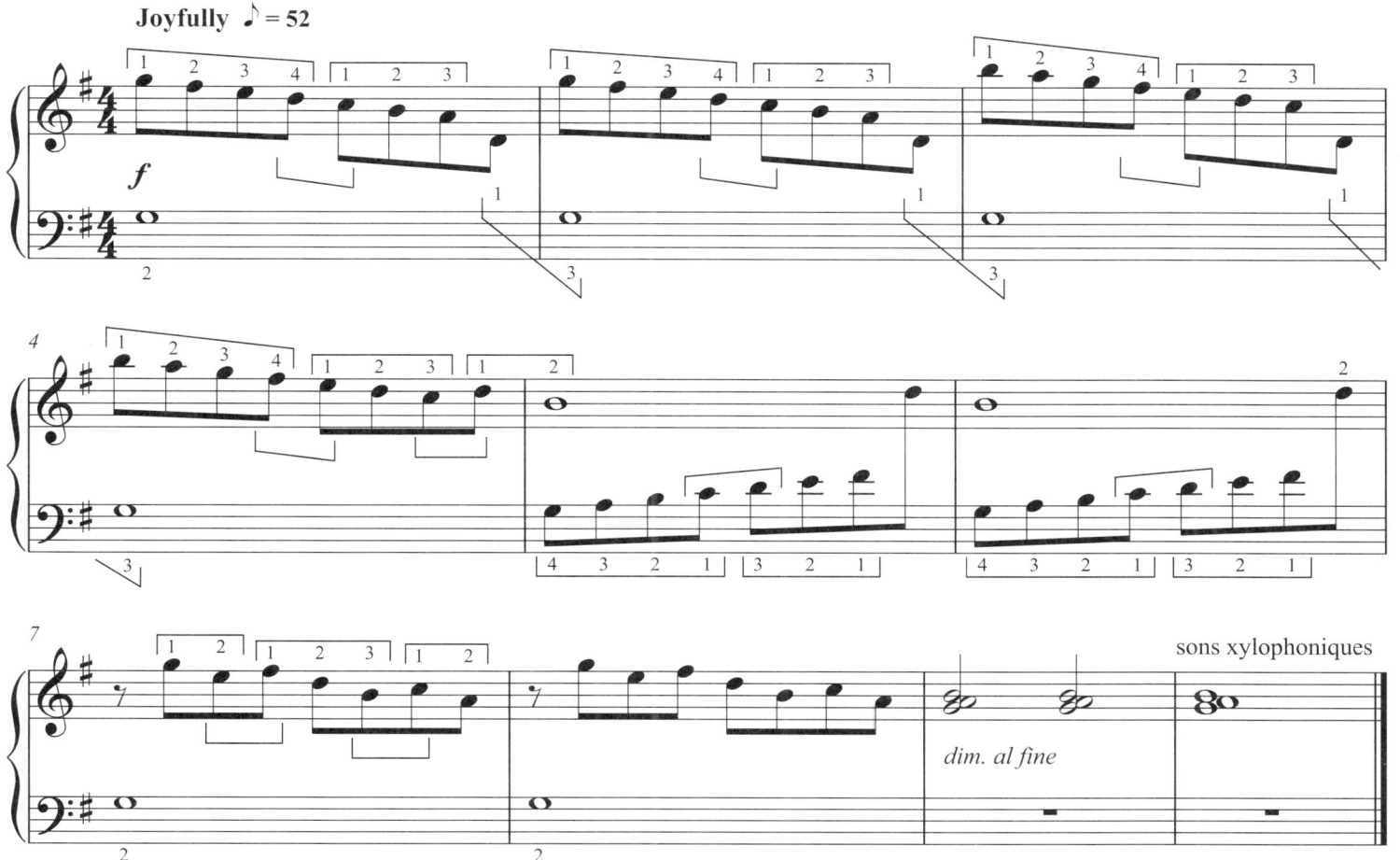

TIP: to create the fade out at the end (as if the wind direction has changed direction making the church bell sound carry to you more faintly), press fingers 2, 3 & 4 of the left hand very lightly on the centre strip at the bottom of the strings being played for the last chord.

The notes should still ring but with a more distant tone.

38. Cogwheels

Add your own musical shaping and dynamics.

TIP: to ensure this flows with even rhythm throughout, replace each hand whilst the other hand plays.

39. Rocking Horse

Add your own dynamics.

These are the same arpeggios which you would encounter in Grade 1 plus a few others with a simple melody attached.

TIP: try to give each arpeggio a nice musical shape and a sense of direction ensuring that the melody sings out at all times.

40. A New Replacement

Aim for a lovely warm ringing sound in this, so make sure you place the fleshy fingertips securely on the strings before releasing them to play each note.

TIP: when you replace the fingers, try to keep your wrist stable.

41. Hymn

Add your own musical shaping and dynamics.

TIP: the melody, shown by the dotted minims, needs to sing out but it needs lovely shaping, so try to decide where the phrases begin and end first. Unless otherwise marked, all of these patterns are played by the thumb and 1st and 2nd fingers.

42. Sailing the Isles

From bar 13, where the melody is in the left hand, it must not be overpowered by the arpeggios in the right hand.

Although there are 3 notes grouped in each hand at the beginning, the 3 crotchet beats in a bar should be clearly heard.

TIP: in bars 1-12 and 21-24 of this study, the direction of the tail indicates which hand is to play, but bars 13-20 show only right-hand notes on the top stave and only left-hand notes on the bottom stave.

43. On Parade

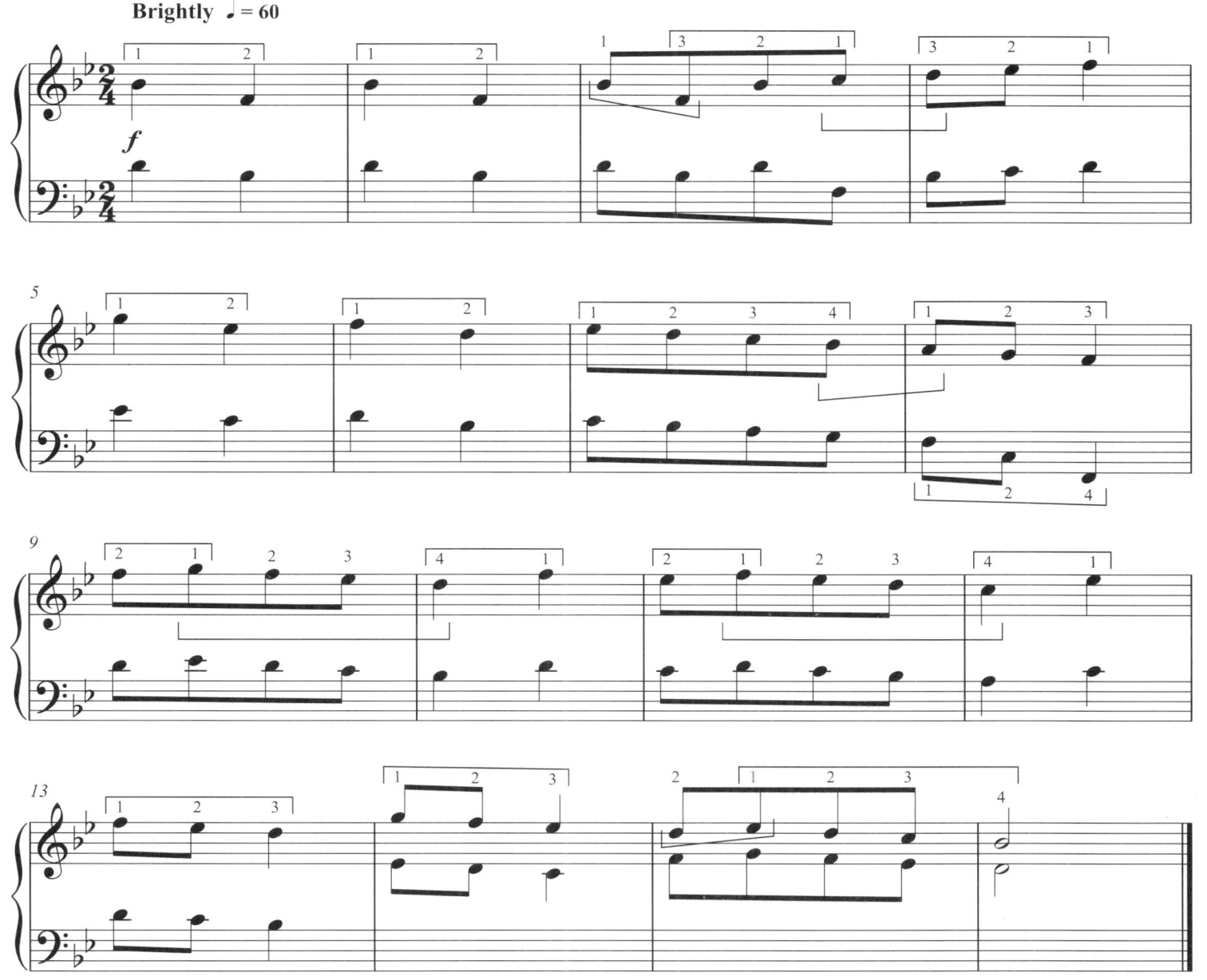

Both hands should sound precisely together and the crotchet pulse should remain steady throughout.

TIP: it is a good idea to replace the fingers pointing down low on the strings before playing the thumb, so you don't get gradually higher up the strings as the piece progresses.

44. The Watermill

The semiquavers are reminiscent of the 'clicky-clacky' sound of the machinery of a watermill. The turn around in the left hand quavers must not delay the beat.

TIP: the golden rule of placing is invaluable in this study i.e. place all the fingers in one direction. The brackets show you how to do this.

N.B. the melody in bars 11 and 13 is not a sequence of bar 5; don't get caught out.

45. Wallabies

If you are playing this for the exam, please keep to the fingering marked. It could be possible to cheat in places and divide between hands, but this exercise is all about turning smoothly in arpeggios.

TIP: draw back the elbow first to lead the right hand up the harp. Replace fingers back lower than the thumb as you turn over. For the swung rhythm, think *Waltzing Matilda* ...

46. Chinese Kites

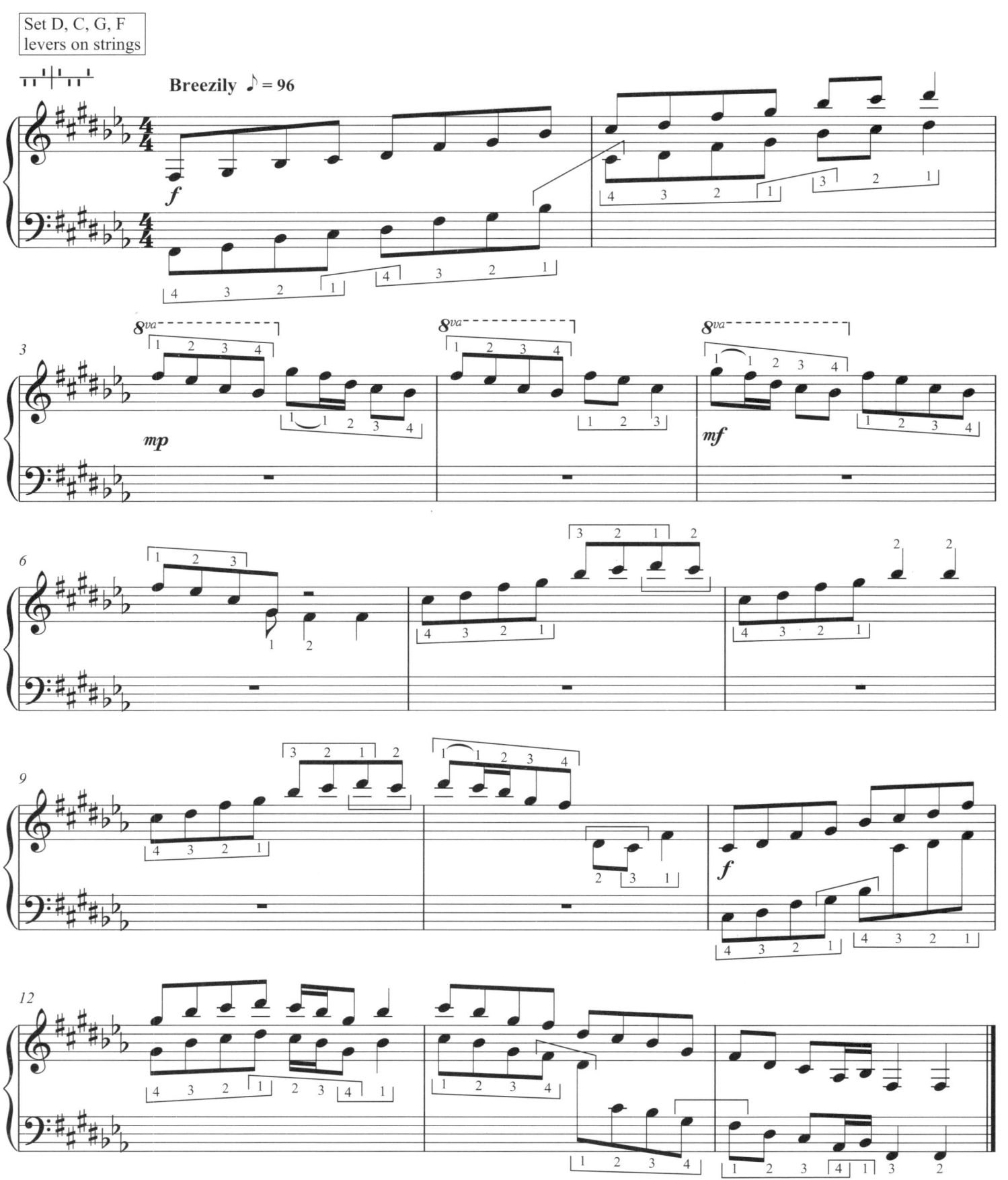

TIP: make sure all the other fingers in the bracket are actually placed on the strings before you slide your thumbs. Keeping your left elbow away from your body allows your left hand to move more freely, especially as it goes up the harp.

47. Scales in the Desert

Lever Harp Only

Keep the scale in the last bar all in the left hand for evenness of tone. Likewise, follow the fingering marked in the first two bars.

TIP: listen out for the octatonic scale (alternating tones and semitones) at the beginning. Make sure that you can play scales smoothly and evenly before you try to co-ordinate the right hand melody.

48. Scales in the Mountains

You might think that C♯ major is a very difficult key, but look at the pedal diagram; does anything strike you? It's just like C major but with all the notes a semitone higher.

TIP: try playing this piece in C major first, and then try it in C♯ major. The higher key was chosen to suit the imagery of the mountains. You could experiment with playing this in C♭ major (with all the pedals in the flat position) and see how much darker it sounds).

49. Camel Ride

This needs to be played in a very deliberate style, to evoke the lumbering camel. It needs very careful co-ordination between the hands, especially in the last bar. Add your own dynamics, as you think best, to help create this image.

TIP: practise the left-hand ostinato pattern until it becomes second nature before you try to combine the two hands.

50. Ditto!

TIP: keep hands close to the strings in order to replace more quickly and place cleanly and firmly to avoid buzzing on repeated notes.

51. Floating

All the fingers need to be even in this study.

TIP: keep your wrist still when playing downwards arpeggiandi so that your 4th finger has to be strong.

52. Goldfish

Harmonics should be clear and singing. Watch for any differences in height on the string between ♮ notes and those which are ♯ on the pedal and very large lever harps, and adjust accordingly the point at which the string needs to be stopped.

The phrasing in this is not quite perhaps what you would expect so try to shape phrases carefully.

TIP: for a more resonant sound, play the first of the 4th-finger notes in each slide, *then* place the other fingers. This puts a little more power into the 4th finger too.

53. Shining Scales

Aim to shape the phrases and produce smooth, even scales. Try practising the scales with different rhythms to throw the accents onto any weaker fingers. Replace the fingers quickly on the repeated Es in the last two bars.

TIP: watch out for the leap and quick replacement of the fingers from the end of bar 6 to the beginning of bar 7.

54. Down Under

Fix E♭ only

The right hand plays the accompaniment to the left hand as soloist in this, so project the left hand well and cleanly.

TIP: for greater clarity in left-hand semiquavers, play them lower on the strings.

55. Cool Dude

This needs to have a good swing groove throughout.

TIP: make sure your left palm dampens absolutely flat against the strings to ensure the étouffé notes really are dampened.

Placing and playing ⌐1 2 3 4⌐ can be tricky. Try to make sure that this is precise.

56. In a Hammock

TIP: sliding the thumb is what captures the swinging hammock feeling. Add your own dynamics.

57. Spooky Strings

Lever harp:
Tune D string above middle C down a semitone

The left hand plays étouffés throughout except at the top of the glissando in bar 8 and the final chord.

TIP: for the right hand staccato notes, replace the fingers lightly on the strings immediately after playing them.

58. Colour Changes

Even though not marked *f* this needs a full, resonant sound.

TIP: for a brittle sound, do not articulate fully, and keep fingers straight.

For the right hand high A harmonic, bring the knuckle of your second finger and tip of the thumb closer together on the strings. The harmonics at the 12th should have the slightly 'untrue' sound of some old bells.

59. Bells

TIP: the hands should be balanced and the fingers even in rhythm and tone. Add your own dynamics to make this more interesting.

60. Elizabeth's Revel

This is a study in right-hand scales and light, repeated, arpeggiated and non-arpeggiated chords. It is pretending to be Elizabethan. There was little music expressly written down for harp for that period. Add your own dynamics.

TIP: try listening to some genuine music for virginals from that period to give you a feeling for the style. Watch out for the descending chord at the end and make sure the bottom note can be heard.

61. Reflections

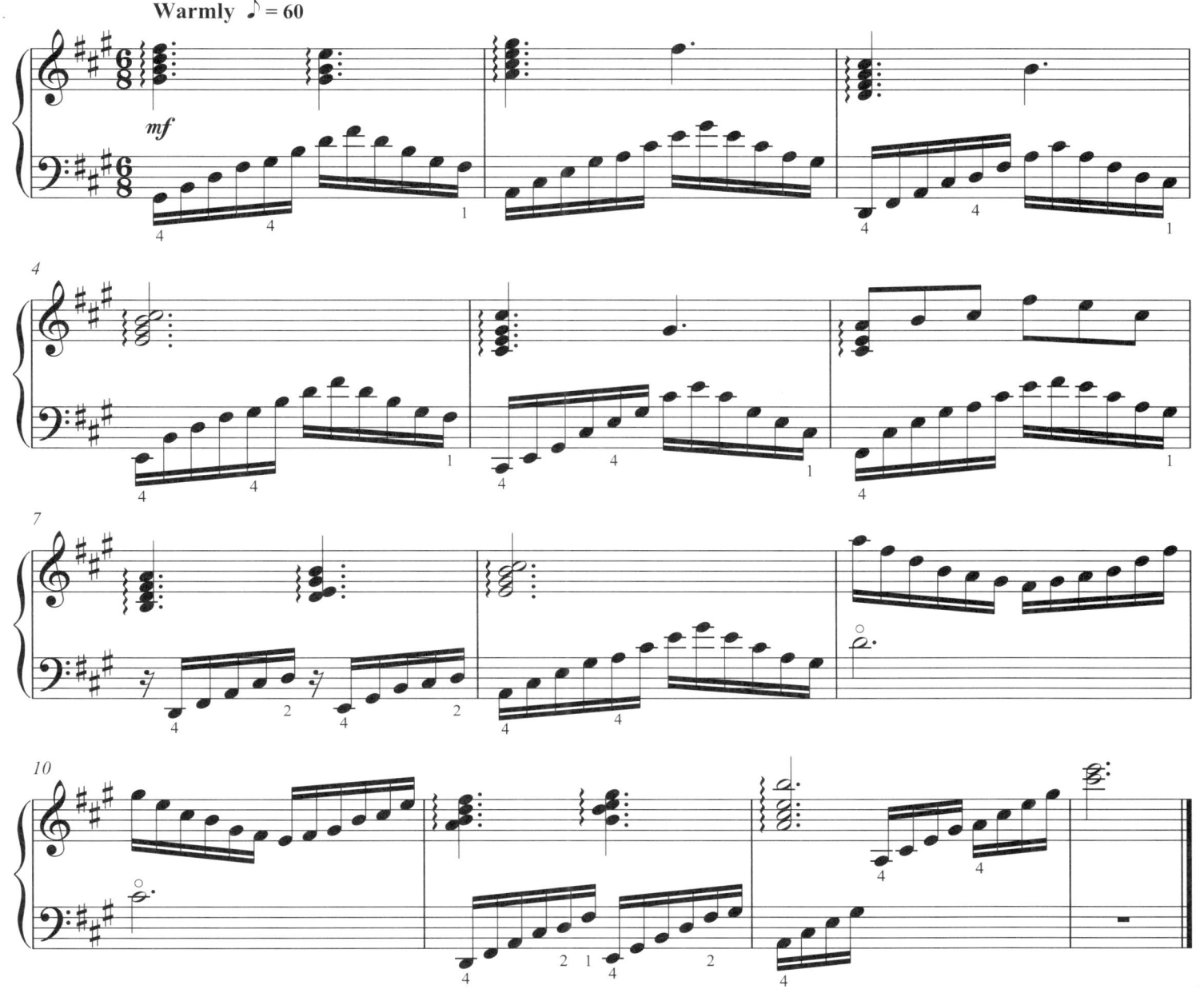

This needs a rich tone throughout.

TIP: because the technical difficulty is in the arpeggios, take care that these do not dominate the melody at the tcp of the spread chords and in the single notes.

62. The Elegant Drawing Room

This Alberti bass study needs to be even and smooth, projecting a lovely radiant, beautifully phrased melody at all times. Add your own dynamics.

TIP: decide on the fingering and placing that is best for you to achieve this – then write it in and stick to it, so your fingers learn the placing patterns.

63. Mind your own Business

This study is for independence of the hands. Add your own dynamics.

TIP: for the staccato notes in the last bar, replace your finger immediately on the string to dampen it.

64. Going East

In this piece, you can choose whether to alternate right and left hand throughout the arpeggios as indicated by the direction of the tails, or to keep all the melody in the right thumb. However you choose to distribute the arpeggios between the hands, the melody should sing out clearly.

TIP: for a more resonant xylophone sound, press only lightly against the soundboard and bottom of the string; for a tighter sound, press more firmly – you choose.

For the pincé notes, if used, play the string between the nails of the 2nd finger and thumb together.

51

65. Lever it Up

Lever Harp Only

Lever changes should not hold up the rhythmic flow here. Add your own dynamics.

TIP: look and plan ahead and use your eye, ear and memory – including muscle (kinaesthetic) memory – combined together to learn to co-ordinate this precisely.

Just before changing the lever, place the finger on the string just played to dampen it so that the lever does not cause a buzz.

66. Pedalling Up and Down Hill

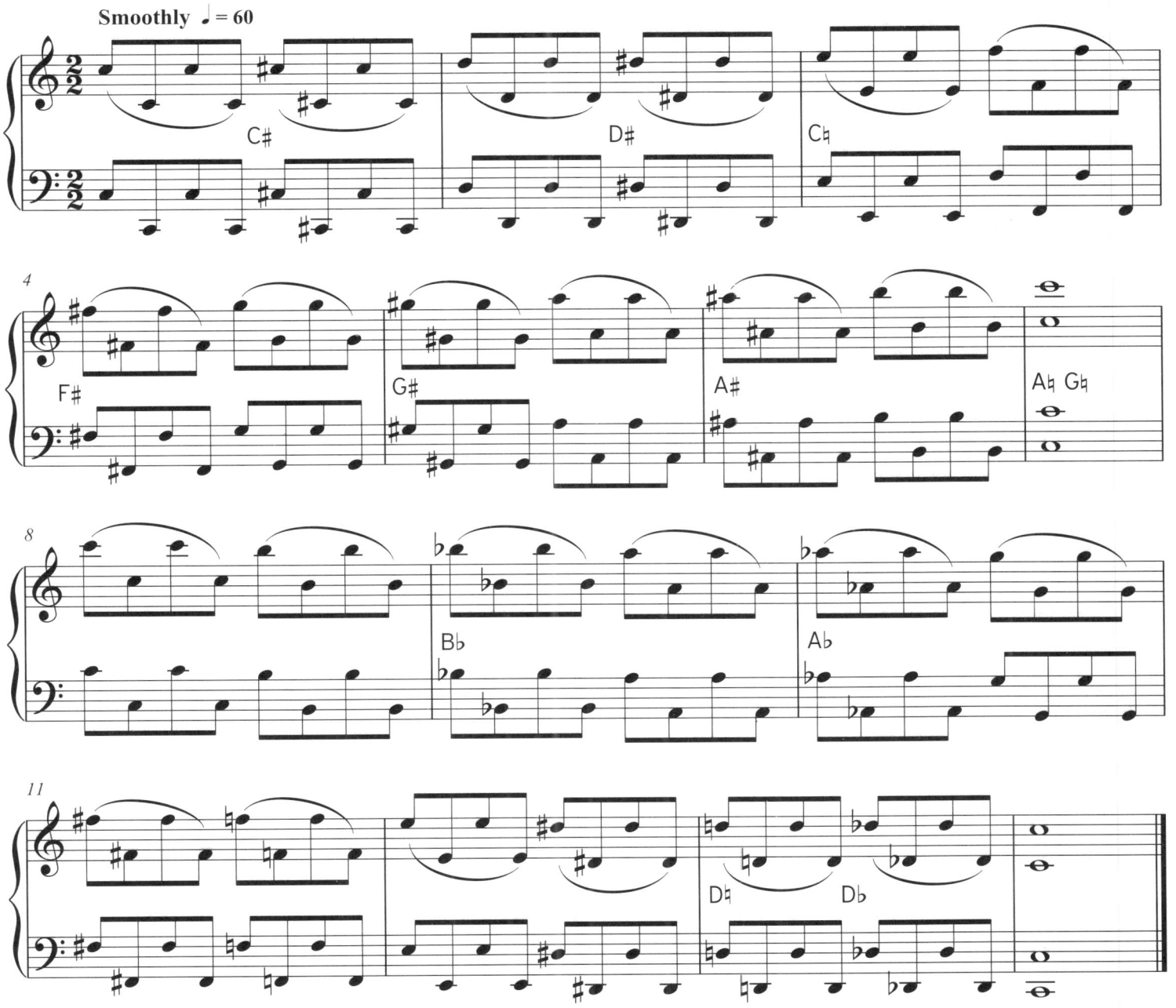

Add your own dynamics.

TIP: for cleaner pedal changes, make sure that you replace your thumb before you move the pedal. It is a good idea from the start to have the toes of the left and right feet waiting to change the C and F pedals.

67. An Ornamental Tune

Add your own musical shaping and dynamics.

TIP: for successful mordents, there needs to be suppleness in the wrist. The melody should project at all times with a light chordal accompaniment.

For security in lever changes, it is worth trying to make each lever change consistently on a quaver beat.

68. Middle of the Irish Sea

This study gets its title because it does not know where it comes from! Could it be Scotland, Ireland, or even Cornwall?

The technical challenge here is in the sliding thumbs.

TIP: aim for a light, even sound with smooth sliding thumbs. Try to keep the thumb knuckle joint stable and not let it bend too far backwards as you start each of these groups.

69. Showing Off!

Chords should be big and lush!

TIP: dividing the trills between the hands makes for ease in playing.
Trills should be even and measured with a clear sense of pulse.

70. A Firm Fist

TIP: to place securely and firmly, the hand needs to be balanced beside the strings – neither pulling the hand up too far towards the thumb, or pulling too far down towards the 4th finger.

If you articulate your fingers for every chord – not just the long ones – see how this improves the sound.

71. Two into One

Lever Harp Only

TIP: notice how, in bar 4 for example, that both lines need to be condensed into the right hand to enable the lever change to be made with the left hand.

72. Chunky Glisses

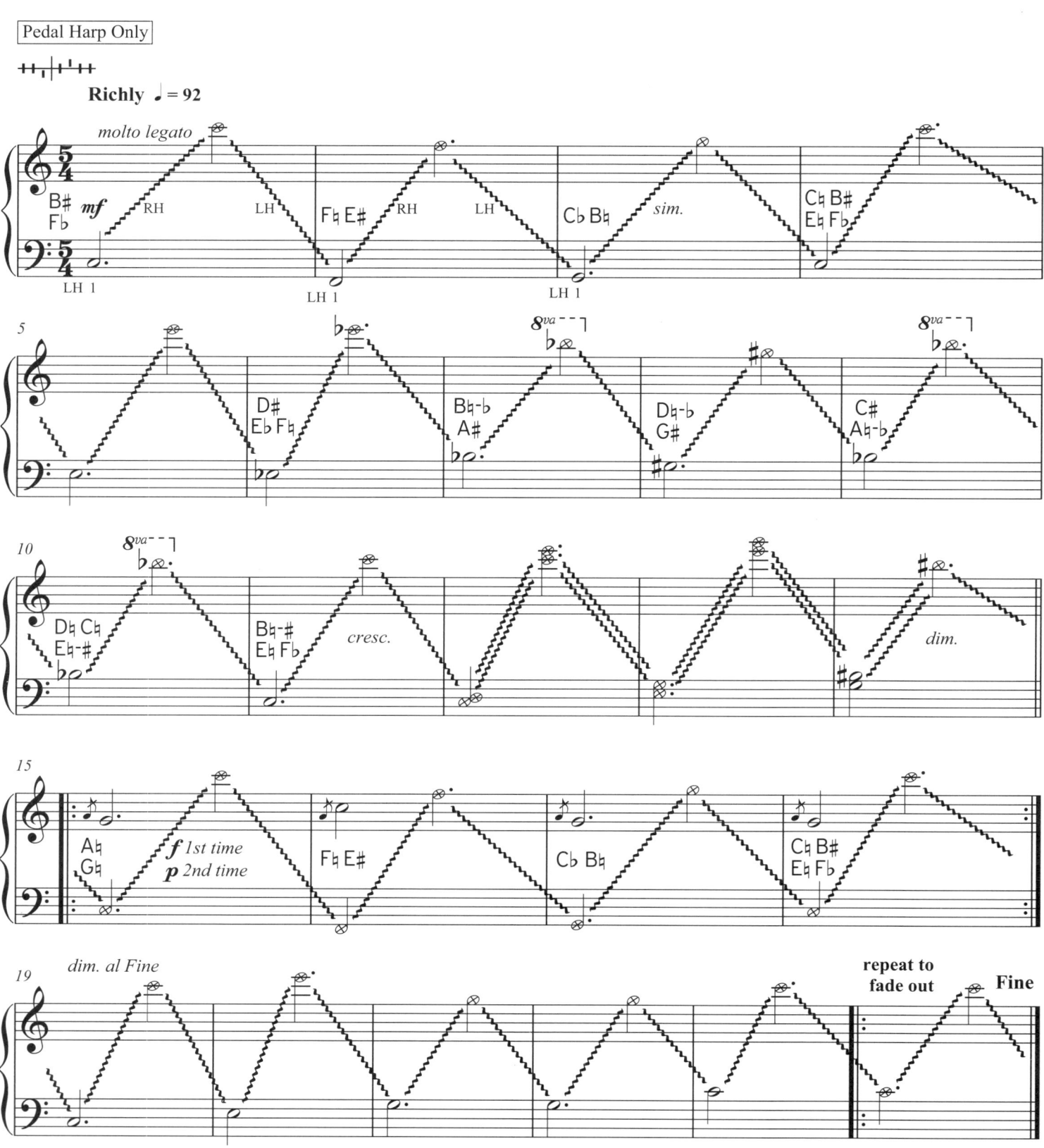

The normal notes indicate that the note should be sounded as a distinct melody note but the circles with crosses are approximate e.g. the first note of each bar until bar 12 where the double glissandi begin should be distinct melody notes. Project the treble clef melody notes from bar 14.

Pedal changes need to be moved quickly and quietly, especially where the pedal affects the first notes of each bar.

TIP: it does not matter if the glissandi do not cover every note down to the last beat of each bar, but rhythmically, it should sound seamless and smooth. It is always quicker and easier to change pedals in a systematic order from left to right, which is what happens where there are four pedal changes here.

N.B. play the repeats in the exam for this study.

73. The Sea

Fix E♭, A♭, D♯ & G♯ levers

Warm and rich tone ♩ = 120

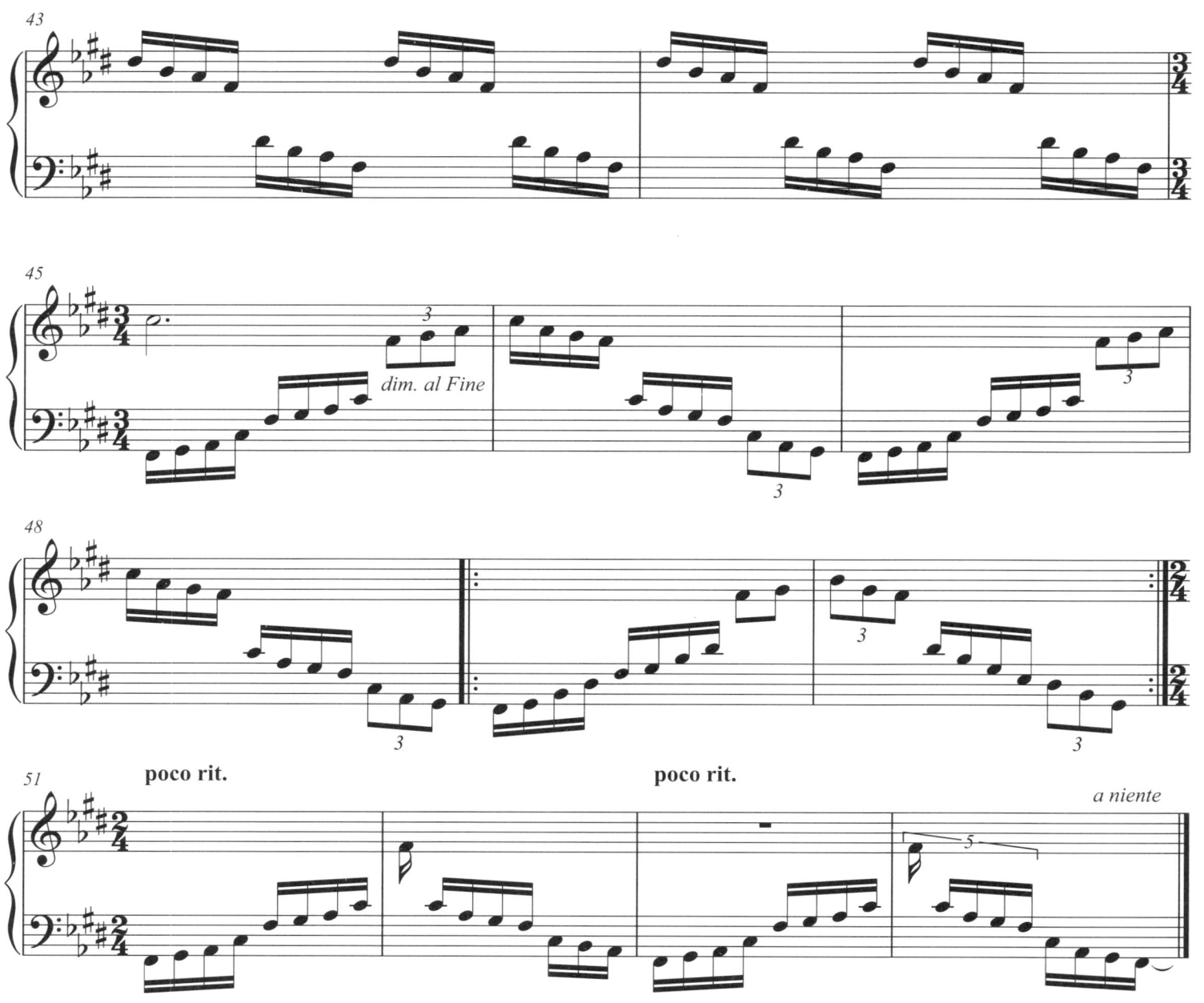

TIP: the direction of the tails indicates which hand plays the notes – tails down = left hand, tails up = right hand.

Grace notes should be played slightly before the beat, with the main note on the beat.

This needs to be rich and warm with washes of harmonic colour.

This page has been left blank to facilitate page-turns

74. Turning & Trilliant

Brilliante ♩ = 92

TIP: the trills are two-handed and, like the title suggests, should sound brilliant.

On the lever harp the changes at bar 28 could be easier if you take the notes of the 2nd–3rd beats in your right hand to give your left hand more time for the changes.

75. Weaving In and Out

Add your own musical shaping.

TIP: lever harpists play with right hand whilst changing levers in bars 6, 8, 10 and 12.

Watch out for the stems in the opposite direction which indicate the melody notes needing to be brought out. They are not the same each time …

76. Paired Bells

TIP: on a pedal or lever harp, you may need to adjust very slightly the position where the string is stopped by the knuckle for the F♯. Aim to create an even ringing sound.

For the high harmonics, the tip of the thumb and knuckle of the forefinger will need to come closer together.

77. Hommage

This is in the style of the harp composers of the late 19th to early 20th centuries, such as Hasselmans, Zabel and Renié. There is also an allusion to Ravel.

TIP: aim for a warm melodic sound in the right thumb, which may be helped by playing a little more into the pad of the thumb tip. Lean the tip of the thumb into the string and then release it. Always imagine the sound you want to produce before you play it.

78. Careful Whisper

This study needs some nifty pedalling control.

TIP: listen to the washes of colour which you are creating here and respond to them sensitively in dynamics and phrasing.

79. I'm a B-Lever

Lever Harp only

* change lever with thumb whilst playing note with 2

Blade harps: change lever with thumb & 2, whilst playing note with 3.

TIP: keep the RH accompaniment light to allow the LH melody to sing through.

80. Very Cross Fingering

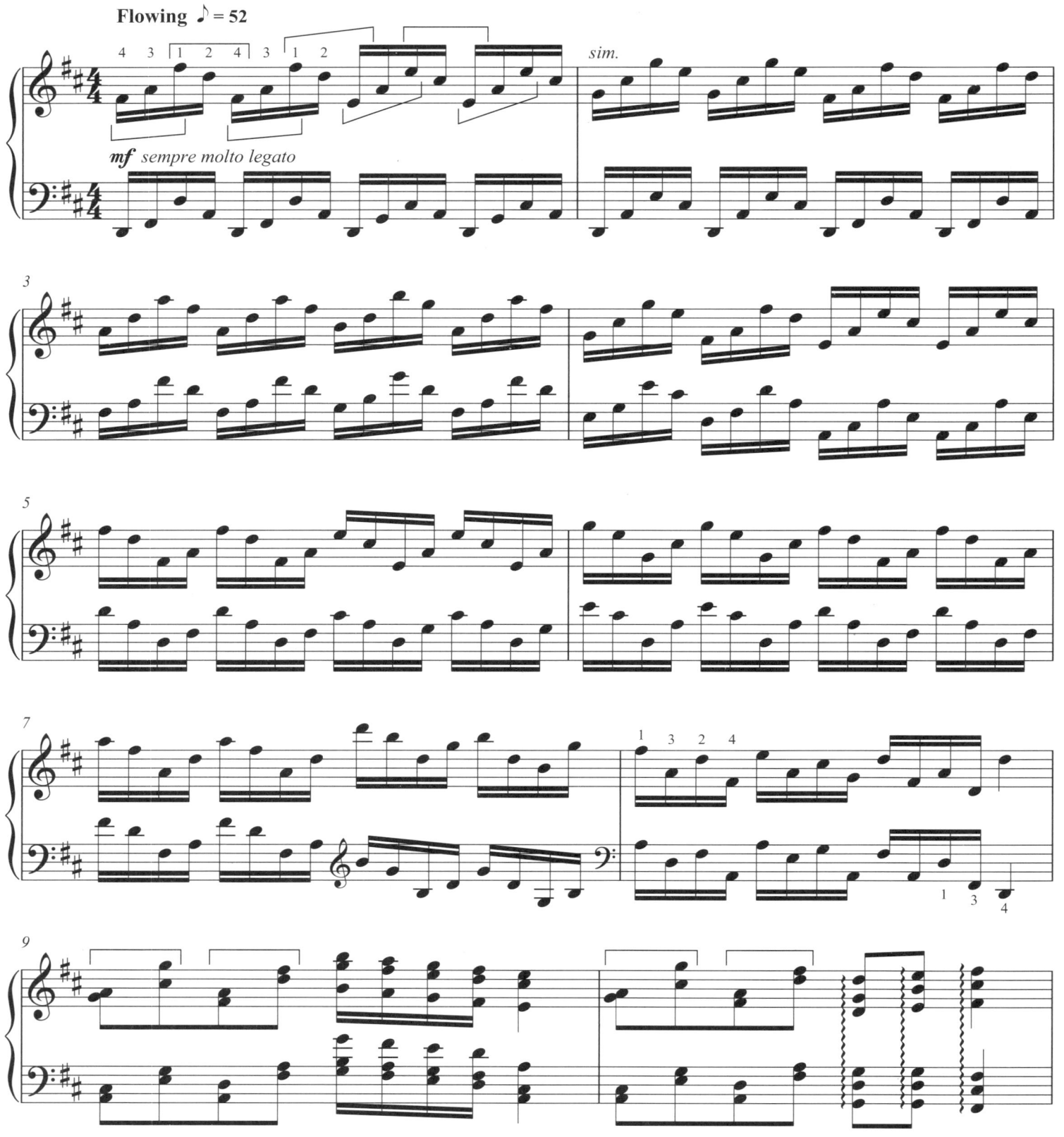

This should be cross-fingered all through, rather than fingering 1313, in bar 11, for example. Think about the beauty of tone throughout.

TIP: this is best achieved with stable hands. Let your fingers do all the work. Articulate, and this will give you clarity of sound.

81. Flashing Levers

Throughout this piece, the right hand only plays the strings, while the left hand only changes the levers.

TIP: the challenge in this study is changing the levers, quickly and precisely at the tempo indicated. Begin practising slowly, then build up the speed as you become more confident at changing the levers. It would be possible to retune or transcribe this piece and avoid going into D♭ major (played enharmonically by the C♯s), but that would take all the fun and skill out of it! For examination purposes, it must be played as written.

On an electric harp, the consecutive chromaticisms (e.g. bars 3-4) may be played as lever slides.

On most acoustic instruments, the string probably needs to be re-sounded.

82. Incy Wincy Slider

TIP: replace fingers on strings to create staccato notes.